# Descending
# Figure

# Louise Glück
# Descending Figure

THE ECCO PRESS

Some of the poems have been published in the following
magazines, to whose editors grateful acknowledgement is made:
*American Poetry Review, Antaeus, Iowa Review, The New
Republic, The New Yorker* ("The Drowned Children" "Illumina-
tions" "Pietà," "Aphrodite," and sections of "Descending
Figure" and "Tango"), *Salmagundi*, and *Water Table*.

I wish to thank the Guggenheim Foundation, the National
Endowment for the Arts, and the Vermont Council for their
support. And for the criticism which has helped to shape these
poems, my special thanks to Ellen Voigt.

—L.G.

*First published by The Ecco Press in 1980*
*100 West Broad Street, Hopewell, NJ 08525*
*Published simultaneously in Canada by*
*Penguin Books Canda Ltd., Ontario*
*Printed in the United States of America*
*The Ecco Press logo by Ahmed Yacoubi*
*Designed by Loretta Li*

Library of Congress Cataloging in Publication Data

Glück, Louise, 1943 –
   Descending figure.
   (The American poetry series; 20)
   I. Title.
PS3557.L8D4      811'.54      80-223
ISBN 0-912-94671-7 (hardbound)
ISBN 0-912-94672-5 (paperback)

Third printing, 1993

FOR MY MOTHER AND FATHER

FOR JOHN

# CONTENTS

# 1 *The Garden*

# THE DROWNED CHILDREN

You see, they have no judgment.
So it is natural that they should drown,
first the ice taking them in
and then, all winter, their wool scarves
floating behind them as they sink
until at last they are quiet.
And the pond lifts them in its manifold dark arms.

But death must come to them differently,
so close to the beginning.
As though they had always been
blind and weightless. Therefore
the rest is dreamed, the lamp,
the good white cloth that covered the table,
their bodies.

And yet they hear the names they used
like lures slipping over the pond:
*What are you waiting for
come home, come home, lost
in the waters, blue and permanent.*

# THE GARDEN

1   *The Fear of Birth*

One sound. Then the hiss and whir
of houses gliding into their places.
And the wind
leafs through the bodies of animals—

But my body that could not content itself
with health—why should it be sprung back
into the chord of sunlight?

It will be the same again.
This fear, this inwardness,
until I am forced into a field
without immunity
even to the least shrub that walks
stiffly out of the dirt, trailing
the twisted signature of its root,
even to a tulip, a red claw.

And then the losses,
one after another,
all supportable.

## 2  *The Garden*

The garden admires you.
For your sake it smears itself with green pigment,
the ecstatic reds of the roses,
so that you will come to it with your lovers.

And the willows—
see how it has shaped these green
tents of silence. Yet
there is still something you need,
your body so soft, so alive, among the stone animals.

Admit that it is terrible to be like them,
beyond harm.

## 3  *The Fear of Love*

That body lying beside me like obedient stone—
once its eyes seemed to be opening,
we could have spoken.

At that time it was winter already.
By day the sun rose in its helmet of fire
and at night also, mirrored in the moon.
Its light passed over us freely,
as though we had lain down
in order to leave no shadows,
only these two shallow dents in the snow.
And the past, as always, stretched before us,
still, complex, impenetrable.

How long did we lie there
as, arm in arm in their cloaks of feathers,
the gods walked down
from the mountain we built for them?

## 4 Origins

As though a voice were saying
*You should be asleep by now—*
But there was no one. Nor
had the air darkened,
though the moon was there,
already filled in with marble.

As though, in a garden crowded with flowers,
a voice had said
*How dull they are, these golds,*
*so sonorous, so repetitious*
until you closed your eyes,
lying among them, all
stammering flame:

And yet you could not sleep,
poor body, the earth
still clinging to you—

5   *The Fear of Burial*

In the empty field, in the morning,
the body waits to be claimed.
The spirit sits beside it, on a small rock—
nothing comes to give it form again.

Think of the body's loneliness.
At night pacing the sheared field,
its shadow buckled tightly around.
Such a long journey.
And already the remote, trembling lights of the village
not pausing for it as they scan the rows.
How far away they seem,
the wooden doors, the bread and milk
laid like weights on the table.

# PALAIS DES ARTS

Love long dormant showing itself:
the large expected gods
caged really, the columns
sitting on the lawn, as though perfection
were not timeless but stationary—that
is the comedy, she thinks,
that they are paralyzed. Or like the matching swans,
insular, circling the pond: restraint so passionate
implies possession. They hardly speak.
On the other bank, a small boy throws bits of bread
into the water. The reflected monument
is stirred, briefly, stricken with light—
She can't touch his arm in innocence again.
They have to give that up and begin
as male and female, thrust and ache.

# PIETA

Under the strained
fabric of her skin, his heart
stirred. She listened,
because he had no father.
So she knew
he wanted to stay
in her body, apart
from the world
with its cries, its
roughhousing,
but already the men
gather to see him
born: they crowd in
or kneel at worshipful
distance, like
figures in a painting
whom the star lights, shining
steadily in its dark context.

# DESCENDING FIGURE

1  *The Wanderer*

At twilight I went into the street.
The sun hung low in the iron sky,
ringed with cold plumage.
If I could write to you
about this emptiness—
Along the curb, groups of children
were playing in the dry leaves.
Long ago, at this hour, my mother stood
at the lawn's edge, holding my little sister.
Everyone was gone; I was playing
in the dark street with my other sister,
whom death had made so lonely.
Night after night we watched the screened porch
filling with a gold, magnetic light.
Why was she never called?
Often I would let my own name glide past me
though I craved its protection.

## 2　*The Sick Child*
—RIJKSMUSEUM

A small child
is ill, has wakened.
It is winter, past midnight
in Antwerp. Above a wooden chest,
the stars shine.
And the child
relaxes in her mother's arms.
The mother does not sleep;
she stares
fixedly into the bright museum.
By spring the child will die.
Then it is wrong, wrong
to hold her—
Let her be alone,
without memory, as the others wake
terrified, scraping the dark
paint from their faces.

3    *For My Sister*

Far away my sister is moving in her crib.
The dead ones are like that,
always the last to quiet.

Because, however long they lie in the earth,
they will not learn to speak
but remain uncertainly pressing against the wooden bars,
so small the leaves hold them down.

Now, if she had a voice,
the cries of hunger would be beginning.
I should go to her;
perhaps if I sang very softly,
her skin so white,
her head covered with black feathers. . . .

# THANKSGIVING

They have come again to graze the orchard,
knowing they will be denied.
The leaves have fallen; on the dry ground
the wind makes piles of them, sorting
all it destroys.

What doesn't move, the snow will cover.
It will give them away; their hooves
make patterns which the snow remembers.
In the cleared field, they linger
as the summoned prey whose part
is not to forgive. They can afford to die.
They have their place in the dying order.

# 2 *The Mirror*

# EPITHALAMIUM

There were others; their bodies
were a preparation.
I have come to see it as that.

As a stream of cries.
So much pain in the world—the formless
grief of the body, whose language
is hunger—

And in the hall, the boxed roses:
what they mean

is chaos. Then begins
the terrible charity of marriage,
husband and wife
climbing the green hill in gold light
until there is no hill,
only a flat plain stopped by the sky.

*Here is my hand,* he said.
But that was long ago.
*Here is my hand that will not harm you.*

# ILLUMINATIONS

### 1

My son squats in the snow in his blue snowsuit.
All around him stubble, the brown
degraded bushes. In the morning air
they seem to stiffen into words.
And, between, the white steady silence.
A wren hops on the airstrip
under the sill, drills
for sustenance, then spreads
its short wings, shadows
dropping from them.

### 2

Last winter he could barely speak.
I moved his crib to face the window:
in the dark mornings
he would stand and grip the bars
until the walls appeared,
calling *light, light,*
that one syllable, in
demand or recognition.

**3**

He sits at the kitchen window
with his cup of apple juice.
Each tree forms where he left it,
leafless, trapped in his breath.
How clear their edges are,
no limb obscured by motion,
as the sun rises
cold and single over the map of language.

# THE MIRROR

Watching you in the mirror I wonder
what it is like to be so beautiful
and why you do not love
but cut yourself, shaving
like a blind man. I think you let me stare
so you can turn against yourself
with greater violence,
needing to show me how you scrape the flesh away
scornfully and without hesitation
until I see you correctly,
as a man bleeding, not
the reflection I desire.

# PORTRAIT

A child draws the outline of a body.
She draws what she can, but it is white all through,
she cannot fill in what she knows is there.
Within the unsupported line, she knows
that life is missing; she has cut
one background from another. Like a child,
she turns to her mother.

And you draw the heart
against the emptiness she has created.

# TANGO

### 1

On evenings like this
twenty years ago:

We sit under the table,
the adults' hands
drum on our heads. Outside,
the street,
the contagious vernacular.

Remember
how we used to dance? Inseparable,
back and forth across the living room,
*Adios Muchachos*, like an insect
moving on a mirror: envy
is a dance, too; the need to hurt
binds you to your partner.

### 2

You thrashed in the crib,
your small mouth circling
the ancient repetitions.
I watched you through the bars,
both of us
actively starving. In the other room
our parents merged into the one
totemic creature:

*Come,* she said. *Come to Mother.*
You stood. You tottered toward
the inescapable body.


3

A dark board covers the sun.
Then the fathers come,
their long cars move slowly down the street,
parting the children. Then
the street is given over to darkness.

The rest follows: the labored
green of the yards, the little gardens
darned with green thread—

The trees also, whose shadows
were blue spokes.

But some the light chooses.
How they tremble
as the moon mounts them, brutal and sisterly:

I used to watch them,
all night absorbed in the moon's neutral silver
until they were finally blurred, disfigured. . . .

4

What was it like to be led?

I trusted no one. My name
was like a stranger's,
read from an envelope.

But nothing was taken from me
that I could have used.
For once, I admit that.

In the hall, posed
for the record's
passionate onset, ages
five and seven:

You were the gold sun on the horizon.
I was the judgment, my shadow
preceded me, not wavering

but like a mold that would be used again.
Your bare feet
became a woman's feet, always
saying two things at once.

Of two sisters
one is always the watcher,
one the dancer.

# SWANS

You were both quiet, looking out over the water.
It was not now; it was years ago,
before you were married.
The sky above the sea had turned
the odd pale peach color of early evening
from which the sea withdrew, bearing
its carved boats: your bodies were like that.
But her face was raised to you,
against the dull waves, simplified
by passion. Then you raised your hand
and from beyond the frame of the dream
swans came to settle on the scaled water.
The sea lay mild as a pool. At its edge,
you faced her, saying
*These are yours to keep*. The horizon burned,
releasing its withheld light.
And then I woke. But for days
when I tried to imagine you leaving your wife
I saw her motionless before your gift:
always the swans glide unmenacing across
the rigid blue of the Pacific Ocean, then rise
in a single wave, pure white and devouring.

# NIGHT PIECE

He knows he will be hurt.
The warnings come to him in bed
because repose threatens him: in the camouflaging
light of the nightlight, he pretends to guard
the flesh in which his life is summarized.
He spreads his arms. On the wall, a corresponding figure
links him to the darkness he cannot control.
In its forms, the beasts originate
who are his enemies. He cannot sleep
apart from them.

# PORTLAND, 1968

You stand as rocks stand
to which the sea reaches
in transparent waves of longing;
they are marred, finally;
everything fixed is marred.
And the sea triumphs,
like all that is false,
all that is fluent and womanly.
From behind, a lens
opens for your body. Why
should you turn? It doesn't matter
who the witness is,
for whom you are suffering,
for whom you are standing still.

# PORCELAIN BOWL

It rules out use:
in a lawn chair, the analogous
body of a woman is arranged,
and in this light
I cannot see what time has done to her.
A few leaves fall. A wind parts the long grass,
making a path going nowhere. And the hand
involuntarily lifts; it moves across her face
so utterly lost—
           The grass sways,
as though that motion were
an aspect of repose.
                 Pearl white
on green. Ceramic
hand in the grass.

# DEDICATION TO HUNGER

1  *From the Suburbs*

They cross the yard
and at the back door
the mother sees with pleasure
how alike they are, father and daughter—
I know something of that time.
The little girl purposefully
swinging her arms, laughing
her stark laugh:

It should be kept secret, that sound.
It means she's realized
that he never touches her.
She is a child; he could touch her
if he wanted to.

## 2  *Grandmother*

"Often I would stand at the window—
your grandfather
was a young man then—
waiting, in the early evening."

That is what marriage is.
I watch the tiny figure
changing to a man
as he moves toward her,
the last light rings in his hair.
I do not question
their happiness. And he rushes in
with his young man's hunger,
so proud to have taught her that:
his kiss would have been
clearly tender—

Of course, of course. Except
it might as well have been
his hand over her mouth.

## 3   *Eros*

To be male, always
to go to women
and be taken back
into the pierced flesh:

         I suppose
memory is stirred.
And the girl child
who wills herself
into her father's arms
likewise loved him
second. Nor is she told
what need to express.
There is a look one sees,
the mouth somehow desperate—

Because the bond
cannot be proven.

## 4   *The Deviation*

It begins quietly
in certain female children:
the fear of death, taking as its form
dedication to hunger,
because a woman's body
*is* a grave; it will accept
anything. I remember
lying in bed at night
touching the soft, digressive breasts,
touching, at fifteen,
the interfering flesh
that I would sacrifice
until the limbs were free
of blossom and subterfuge: I felt
what I feel now, aligning these words—
it is the same need to perfect,
of which death is the mere byproduct.

5   *Sacred Objects*

Today in the field I saw
the hard, active buds of the dogwood
and wanted, as we say, to capture them,
to make them eternal. That is the premise
of renunciation: the child,
having no self to speak of,
comes to life in denial—

I stood apart in that achievement,
in that power to expose
the underlying body, like a god
for whose deed
there is no parallel in the natural world.

# HAPPINESS

A man and woman lie on a white bed.
It is morning. I think
*Soon they will waken.*
On the bedside table is a vase
of lilies; sunlight
pools in their throats.
I watch him turn to her
as though to speak her name
but silently, deep in her mouth—
At the window ledge,
once, twice,
a bird calls.
And then she stirs; her body
fills with his breath.

I open my eyes; you are watching me.
Almost over this room
the sun is gliding.
*Look at your face*, you say,
holding your own close to me
to make a mirror.
How calm you are. And the burning wheel
passes gently over us.

# 3 Lamentations

# AUTUMNAL

Public sorrow, the acquired
gold of the leaf, the falling off,
the prefigured burning of the yield:
which is accomplished. At the lake's edge,
the metal pails are full vats of fire.
So waste is elevated
into beauty. And the scattered dead
unite in one consuming vision of order.
In the end, everything is bare.
Above the cold, receptive earth
the trees bend. Beyond,
the lake shines, placid, giving back
the established blue of heaven.
                    The word
is *bear*: you give and give, you empty yourself
into a child. And you survive
the automatic loss. Against inhuman landscape,
the tree remains a figure for grief; its form
is forced accommodation. At the grave,
it is the woman, isn't it, who bends,
the spear useless beside her.

# AUBADE

Today above the gull's call
I heard you waking me again
to see that bird, flying
so strangely over the city,
not wanting
to stop, wanting
the blue waste of the sea—

Now it skirts the suburb,
the noon light violent against it:

I feel its hunger
as your hand inside me,

a cry
so common, unmusical—

Ours were not
different. They rose
from the unexhausted
need of the body

fixing a wish to return:
the ashen dawn, our clothes
not sorted for departure.

# APHRODITE

A woman exposed as rock
has this advantage:
she controls the harbor.
Ultimately, men appear,
weary of the open.
So terminates, they feel,
a story. In the beginning,
longing. At the end, joy.
In the middle, tedium.

In time, the young wife
naturally hardens. Drifting
from her side, in imagination,
the man returns not to a drudge
but to the goddess he projects.

On a hill, the armless figure
welcomes the delinquent boat,
her thighs cemented shut, barring
the fault in the rock.

# ROSY

When you walked in with your suitcase, leaving
the door open so the night showed
in a black square behind you, with its little stars
like nailheads, I wanted to tell you
you were like the dog that came to you by default,
on three legs: now that she is again no one's,
she pursues her more durable relationships
with traffic and cold nature, as though at pains
to wound herself so that she will not heal.
She is past being taken in by kindness,
preferring wet streets: what death claims
it does not abandon.
You understand, the animal means nothing to me.

# THE DREAM OF MOURNING

I sleep so you will be alive,
it is that simple.
The dreams themselves are nothing.
They are the sickness you control,
nothing more.

I rush toward you in the summer twilight,
not in the real world, but in the buried one
where you are waiting,
as the wind moves over the bay, toying with it,
forcing thin ridges of panic—

And then the morning comes, demanding prey.
Remember? And the world complies.

Last night was different.
Someone fucked me awake; when I opened my eyes
it was over, all the need gone
by which I knew my life.
And for one instant I believed I was entering
the stable dark of the earth
and thought it would hold me.

# THE GIFT

Lord, You may not recognize me
speaking for someone else.
I have a son. He is
so little, so ignorant.
He likes to stand
at the screen door, calling
*oggie, oggie*, entering
language, and sometimes
a dog will stop and come up
the walk, perhaps
accidentally. May he believe
this is not an accident?
At the screen
welcoming each beast
in love's name, Your emissary.

# WORLD BREAKING APART

I look out over the sterile snow.
Under the white birch tree, a wheelbarrow.
The fence behind it mended. On the picnic table,
mounded snow, like the inverted contents of a bowl
whose dome the wind shapes. The wind,
with its impulse to build. And under my fingers,
the square white keys, each stamped
with its single character. I believed
a mind's shattering released
the objects of its scrutiny: trees, blue plums in a bowl,
a man reaching for his wife's hand
across a slatted table, and quietly covering it,
as though his will enclosed it in that gesture.
I saw them come apart, the glazed clay
begin dividing endlessly, dispersing
incoherent particles that went on
shining forever. I dreamed of watching that
the way we watched the stars on summer evenings,
my hand on your chest, the wine
holding the chill of the river. There is no such light.
And pain, the free hand, changes almost nothing.
Like the winter wind, it leaves
settled forms in the snow. Known, identifiable—
except there are no uses for them.

# THE RETURN

At first when you went away
I was frightened; then
a boy touched me on the street,
his eyes were level with mine,
clear and grieving: I
called him in; I spoke to him
in our language,
but his hands were yours,
so gently making their murderous claim—
And then it didn't matter
which one of you I called,
the wound was that deep.

# LAMENTATIONS

1   *The Logos*

They were both still,
the woman mournful, the man
branching into her body.

But god was watching.
They felt his gold eye
projecting flowers on the landscape.

Who knew what he wanted?
He was god, and a monster.
So they waited. And the world
filled with his radiance,
as though he wanted to be understood.

Far away, in the void that he had shaped,
he turned to his angels.

## 2   *Nocturne*

A forest rose from the earth.
O pitiful, so needing
God's furious love—

Together they were beasts.
They lay in the fixed
dusk of his negligence;
from the hills, wolves came, mechanically
drawn to their human warmth,
their panic.

Then the angels saw
how He divided them:
the man, the woman, and the woman's body.

Above the churned reeds, the leaves let go
a slow moan of silver.

3 *The Covenant*

Out of fear, they built a dwelling place.
But a child grew between them
as they slept, as they tried
to feed themselves.

They set it on a pile of leaves,
the small discarded body
wrapped in the clean skin
of an animal. Against the black sky
they saw the massive argument of light.

Sometimes it woke. As it reached its hands
they understood they were the mother and father,
there was no authority above them.

### 4   *The Clearing*

Gradually, over many years,
the fur disappeared from their bodies
until they stood in the bright light
strange to one another.
Nothing was as before.
Their hands trembled, seeking
the familiar.

Nor could they keep their eyes
from the white flesh
on which wounds would show clearly
like words on a page.

And from the meaningless browns and greens
at last God arose, His great shadow
darkening the sleeping bodies of His children,
and leapt into heaven.

How beautiful it must have been,
the earth, that first time
seen from the air.